Paper Folding for
Secret Agents

Origami
X

Nick Robinson &
Paul Harrison

D1441742

CAPSTONE PRESS
a capstone imprint

First U.S. edition published in 2013 by Capstone Press, a Capstone imprint.

Copyright © Ivy Press Limited 2012

This book was conceived, designed, and produced by

Ivy Press
210 High Street
Lewes
East Sussex BN7 2NS
www.ivypress.co.uk

All inquiries should be addressed to:
Capstone Press
1710 Rose Crest Drive
North Mankato, Minnesota 56003
www.capstonepub.com

Library of Congress Cataloging-in-Publication Data
Cataloging-in-publication information is on file with
the Library of Congress

ISBN 978-1-4296-9851-1

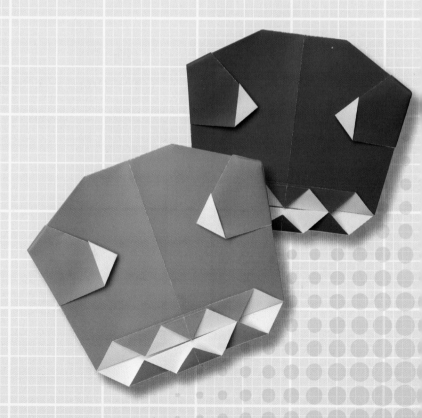

CONTENTS

YOUR MISSION

Congratulations! You have been selected as our new trainee agent. This is your training manual—keep it hidden and keep it safe. Never let it fall into the enemy's hands.

WHAT YOU NEED TO DO

You are to keep your eyes and ears open and report any unusual behavior that you see. You will need to go undercover to avoid being detected. You will be posing as an origami artist.

WHAT YOU NEED TO KNOW

Origami is the art of paper folding. Your training manual provides information on all the skills you will need to learn origami.

As well as looking the part, you will use your folded paper models as the means of passing on messages. Write in code on the paper provided; make an origami model, then pass it on to your contact.

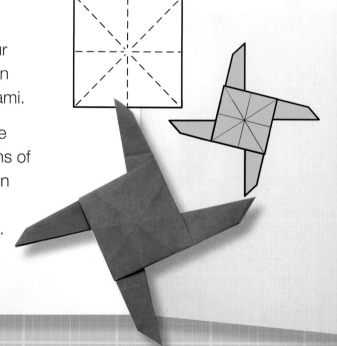

Your contact will be another agent who will make him or herself known using a password. Passwords can be found in your training manual.

Your training manual also contains all the information you need to become a superspy. Inside you will learn different types of codes and ciphers, spying techniques, and how to make useful equipment.

Finally, there is a coded message running along the bottom of some of the pages in your training manual. Make this your motto for your mission. Decode the message using the techniques you have learned from the manual.

CODE 1 (page 10): Cipher wheel
CODE 2 (page 18): Rail fence cipher (3-line)
CODE 3 (page 22): Morse Code
CODE 4 (page 26): Mirror writing
CODE 5 (page 34): Symbol cipher
CODE 6 (page 38): Caesar cipher (+3)

Good luck—and don't get caught.

ORIGAMI BASICS

Origami comes from the words *ori* (paper) and *kami* (folding) and is an art form that has been carried out for hundreds of years. The art of origami is to create models by folding paper.

When you first start paper folding, try to learn the symbols used in the origami steps. This will help you fold the models more easily.

VALLEY FOLD

A black arrow tells you to fold upward.

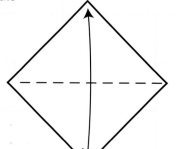

FOLD AND UNFOLD

A black and white arrow tells you to fold and unfold to create a crease.

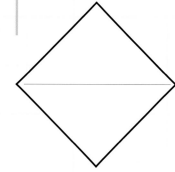

MOUNTAIN FOLD

A curved arrow tells you to fold behind.

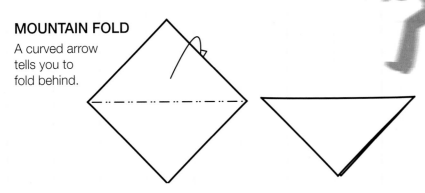

TURN OVER

A curly arrow tells you to turn over.

REPEAT STEPS

A crossed arrow x3 tells you to repeat 3 times on the other side.

x3

PUSH INSIDE

A short black arrow tells you to push the paper inside.

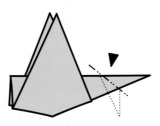 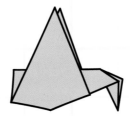

TIPS

PAPER: The paper you find at the back of this book is crisp and brightly colored. Make your models first using "ordinary" paper. Practice on squares of photocopy paper until you can make your model well. Then choose a colored sheet to fold your best work for your mission.

FOLDING TECHNIQUES: Try to fold on a table and with good lighting. Always fold slowly and with care, making each crease nice and sharp before moving on to the next step. Working carefully will guarantee your mission remains top secret!

YOUR MESSAGE: When you have a top-secret message to send or pass on, you should write it on your origami paper (in code, if you need to) then fold it in as you are making your model.

THE EYE

A good spy must always keep his eyes alert. A blink from a spy can pass information to other spies without using words. Once you have folded this origami shape, you can move the flaps at the back to make the eye open and close.

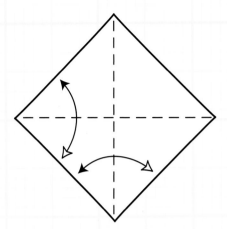

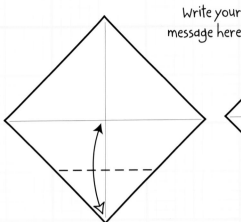

Write your message here

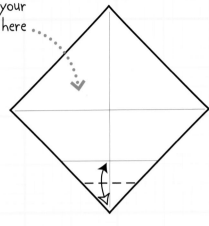

1 Start white side up. Fold corner to opposite corner, crease and unfold. Repeat in the other direction.

2 Fold the lower corner to the center, crease, and unfold.

3 Fold the lower corner to the most recent crease, crease, and unfold.

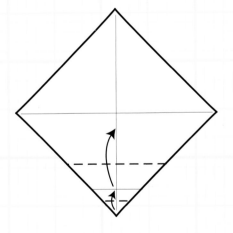

4 Fold the lower corner to the most recent crease. Now fold in on the crease made in step 2.

WHAT IS MORSE CODE?

A code is a message where the letters have been changed for symbols. Morse code is a famous code that uses short and long signals—dots and dashes—instead of letters.

Invented by Samuel Morse in the 1840s, the Morse code wasn't meant for spies to use. Morse's plan was to use it with his other new gadget—the telegraph, which was invented just before the telephone.

When it is dark, use a flashlight to send short or long flashes of light instead of dots and dashes. See page 11 for the Morse code alphabet and give it a try.

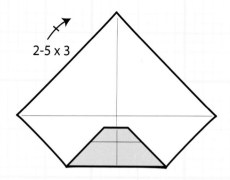

5 This is the result. Repeat steps 2–5 on the other three corners.

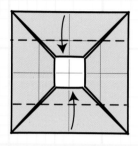

6 Fold the upper and lower edges into the center.

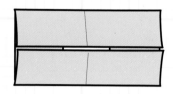

7 This is the result. Turn the model over.

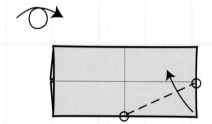

8 Fold the right corner up between the circled points.

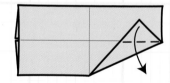

9 Fold the corner down again along the crease that runs across the flap underneath.

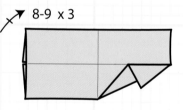

10 Repeat steps 8–9 on the three other corners.

CODE 1   Z FNNC ROX

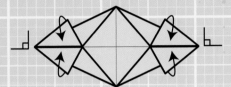

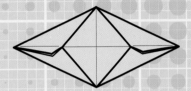

11 Fold the small flaps over so they can be held together.

12 This is the result.

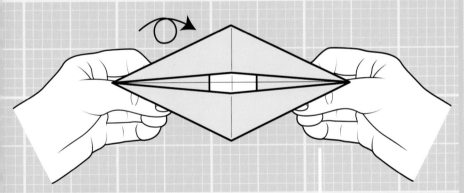

13 Turn the paper over. Hold the finished model by the flaps and move your hands slightly from side to side so the eye opens and closes. Draw an eye to make it more realistic.

MORSE CODE ALPHABET

Keep a copy of this with you at all times—you never know when you might need it.

A ●▬
B ▬●●●
C ▬●▬●
D ▬●●
E ●
F ●●▬●
G ▬▬●
H ●●●●
I ●●
J ●▬▬▬
K ▬●▬
L ●▬●●
M ▬▬
N ▬●
O ▬▬▬
P ●▬▬●
Q ▬▬●▬
R ●▬●
S ●●●
T ▬
U ●●▬
V ●●●▬
W ●▬▬
X ▬●●▬
Y ▬●▬▬
Z ▬▬●●

THE STAR

This is a Japanese shuriken, also known as a throwing star and a ninja star. A shuriken should be hidden before it is thrown. Try to spin it!

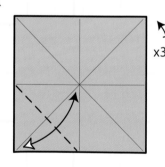

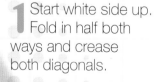

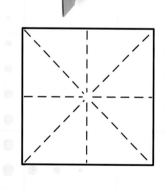

1 Start white side up. Fold in half both ways and crease both diagonals.

2 Turn the paper over and fold a corner to the center, crease, and unfold. Repeat three times.

THE CAESAR CIPHER

A cipher replaces the letters of your message with other letters. One of the most basic is the shift cipher—also known as the Caesar cipher—perhaps invented by the Roman emperor Julius Caesar.

The shift cipher works by using the letters a set number of places (such as +3) down the alphabet. For example, a Caesar Cipher of +3 would look like this:

normal alphabet

A B C D E F G H I J K L M N O P Q R S T U V W X Y Z

D E F G H I J K L M N O P Q R S T U V W X Y Z A B C

Caesar cipher +3

So "COW" would become "FRZ"

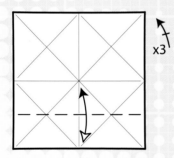

3 Fold the lower edge to the center, crease, and unfold. Repeat three times.

x3

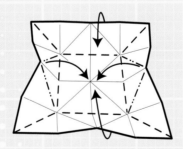

4 Fold the center of the left and right sides into the middle. Let the upper edges fold in, forming points at either end.

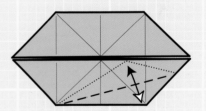

5 Fold the lower right corner to match the dotted line, then unfold.

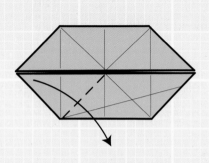

6 Fold the lower left flap downward.

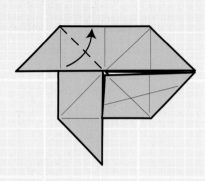

7 Fold the upper left flap upward.

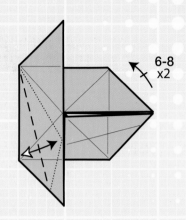

6-8 x2

8 Repeat step 5, then repeat steps 6–8 two more times.

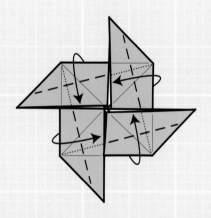

9 Fold the flaps over in turn. You'll need to temporarily undo the first to complete the last.

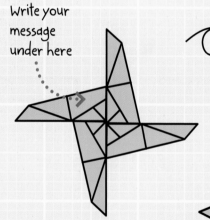

Write your message under here

10 This is the result.

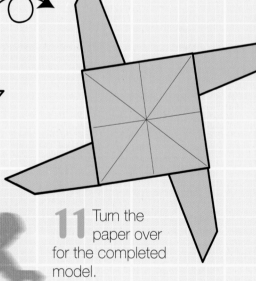

11 Turn the paper over for the completed model.

MAKE AND USE A CIPHER WHEEL

The cipher wheel was invented in Italy in the 15th century and is an easy way to encrypt or decode a message.

YOU WILL NEED: • Two circles of paper, one smaller than the other • paper fastener

1 Write the alphabet around the outside of each circle. The inner circle can either be in alphabetical order or mixed up. If the letters are mixed up make sure all the letters are used. Letters should be evenly spaced.

2 Attach the small circle on top of the large one with a paper fastener at the center point, so you can spin each of the circles on their own. Your cipher wheel is now ready!

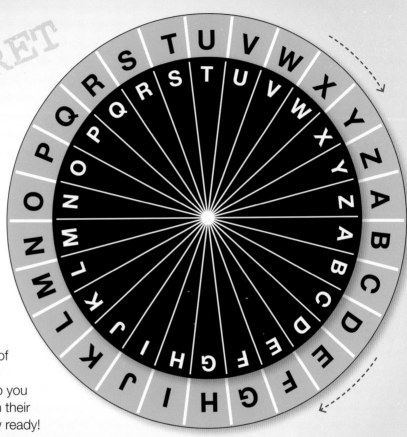

To use your wheel choose a letter to create your code. If you choose "z," then turn the smaller center wheel until "z" is in line with the "a" of the outer wheel. When you write your message, find each letter first on the large circle, then write down the letter in code from the small circle. Your contact should have an identical wheel set to the same position as you. They must find each letter on the large circle and then write down the matching letter from the small circle.

NAVIGATOR

Finding your way around when stranded in a strange land is vitally important. You may not be able to use a GPS system, so a compass to find your way will be very helpful.

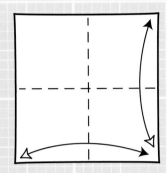

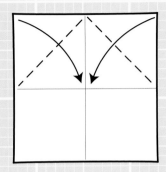

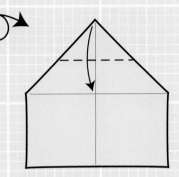

1 Start white side up. Fold in half from side to side, unfold, and repeat the other way.

2 Fold the top two corners to the center.

3 Turn over and fold the top corner to the center.

PASSWORDS

Face-to-face meetings are always a tense situation for a spy. How do you know the people you are meeting are who they say they are? How do you know you're all on the same side? Sometimes passwords are the answer.

Agree some words or phrases that only you and your fellow agents know. Have some fun with them. Here are some examples:

AGENT 1: The Moon is out in Latvia.
AGENT 2: So you must put your sunglasses on.
Or
AGENT 1: The geese are flying backward.
AGENT 2: And the horses are doing the tango.

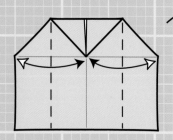

4 Fold the sides to the center, crease, and unfold. Turn the paper over.

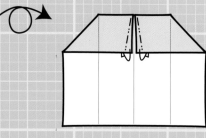

5 Fold two edges a little way underneath, at a slight angle.

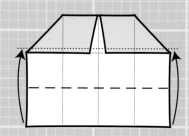

6 Fold the lower edge to the dotted line, slightly past the colored edge.

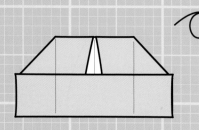

7 This is the result.

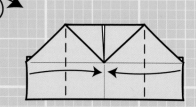

8 Turn the paper over. Fold the sides to the center.

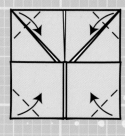

9 Fold all four corners in.

CODE 2

NRSGEEGTCUHVEAT

MIRROR WRITING

Mirror writing is a simple way of concealing a secret message. It has been a popular method for hiding what you are writing about for centuries. In the 1500s the famous Italian painter and inventor, Leonardo da Vinci, used mirror writing in all of his journals.

With some practice, mirror writing is quite easy to do. You simply have to write backward. To read the message, your contact must use a mirror to see the letters the right way. However, don't forget the code may be easy for the enemy to crack too!

Mirror writing looks like this.

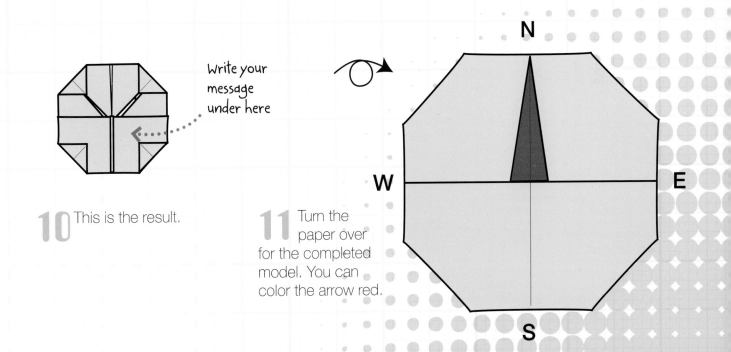

Write your message under here

10 This is the result.

11 Turn the paper over for the completed model. You can color the arrow red.

DEATH MARK

The symbol of a skull can mean death. It can be used to warn you that a substance is poisonous or highly toxic. It is also the sign of your enemies!

grrrrrrrr

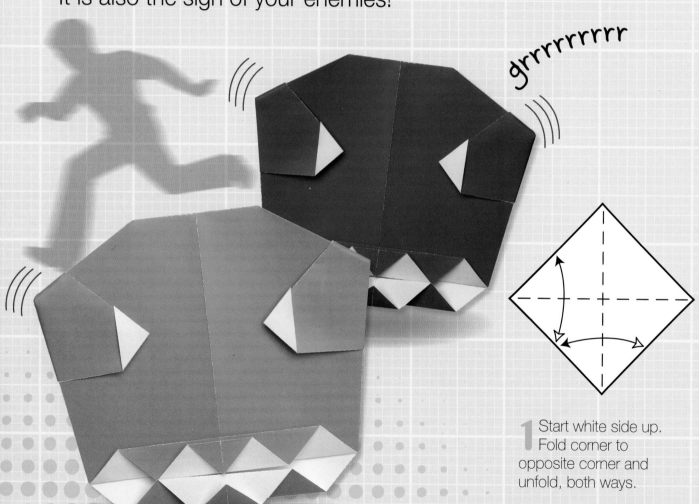

1 Start white side up. Fold corner to opposite corner and unfold, both ways.

SYMBOL CIPHER

The symbol cipher uses symbols rather than letters. You can have some fun designing your own alphabet of symbols—just make sure your contact has the key to what the symbols mean!

An example of a symbol cipher alphabet

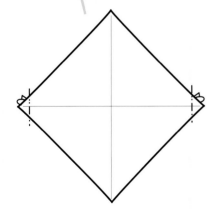

2 Fold behind the tips of the two opposite corners in the middle.

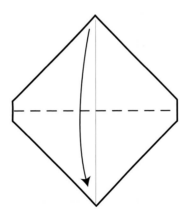

3 Fold in half from top to bottom.

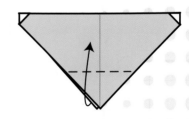

4 Fold up two layers at the point.

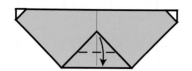

5 Fold both layers down again.

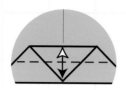

6 Fold both layers in half, then unfold.

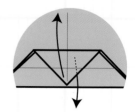

7 Lift up the first layer, then fold down the lower layer.

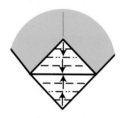

8 Make a series of folds to form the teeth. Pleat the layers to make a pattern.

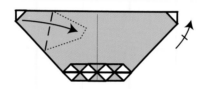

9 Fold the left corner in to match the dotted line. Repeat on the right.

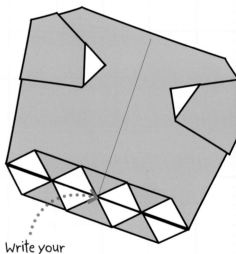

Write your message under here

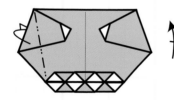

10 Fold the left corner behind. Repeat on the right.

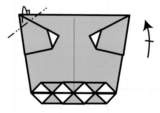

11 Fold the top left corner behind. Repeat on the right.

12 This creates the completed model.

■ ●●●/●● ━/━● ●━━●/●/━━●/●/━━●/●●●/●/●━ ●

BODY LANGUAGE

How well you can find things out will tell you whether you will be a successful spy or not. You may not be told top-secret information, but a good spy knows that you can find out important things in other ways.

You can learn a lot just by watching what people do during a conversation— this is called reading their body language.

Scratching their nose
Person might be lying

Blinking a lot
Person might be lying

Avoiding eye contact
Person might be nervous

Crossed arms
Person is being defensive

Drumming fingers
Person is anxious

Leaning forward
Person is interested in what you are saying

Leaning backward
Person is feeling threatened

Fiddling with an object
Person is bored or not paying attention

SPY PLANE

Spies need to travel to all parts of the globe to carry out their work. They also need to go there very fast! This sleek design is perfect for the job.

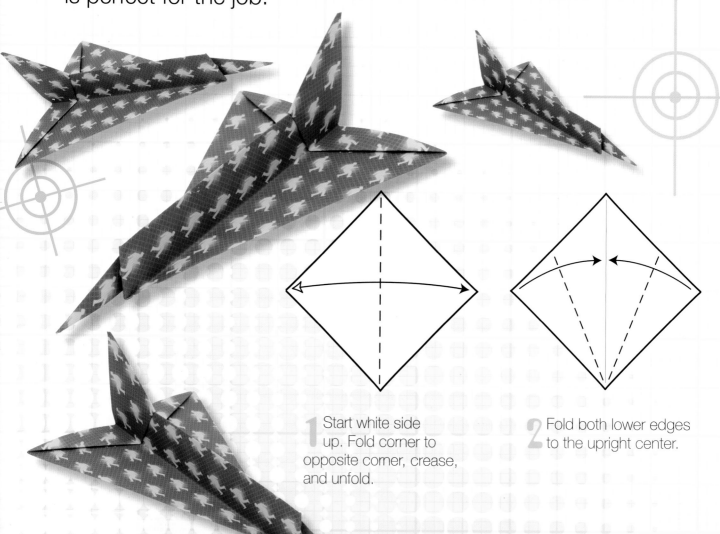

1 Start white side up. Fold corner to opposite corner, crease, and unfold.

2 Fold both lower edges to the upright center.

SEEING AROUND CORNERS

Being able to observe things without being seen yourself is one of the top skills a spy needs to learn. Many spies have wished they could see around corners, but it's quite easy to do so with a few basic bits of equipment.

YOU WILL NEED • A small mirror • a stick • some garden wire • some heavy-duty tape

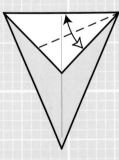

This end is the handle.

Back of mirror

Hold the mirror out around the corner and you can see what is going on without anybody seeing you.

Bend the wire along the bottom of the stick, and keep in place with tape.

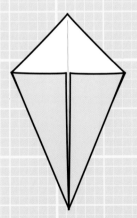

3 This is the result. Turn the paper over.

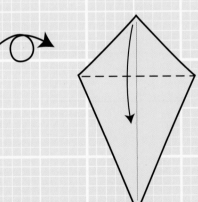

4 Fold the upper triangular flap down.

5 Fold the lower right white edge to the top edge, crease, and unfold.

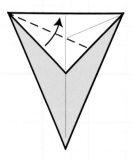

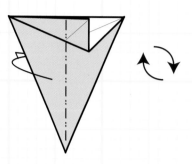

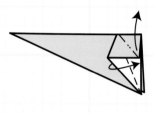

6 Make the same fold on the other side, but leave it in place.

7 Fold the left half underneath and rotate the paper 90 degrees.

8 Pull the colored corner upward as you fold the white edge to the right.

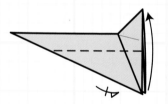

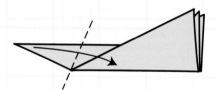

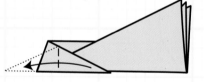

9 Fold the tip of the wing to the top of the tail. Repeat the fold on the other side.

10 Fold the lower edge of the nose over to lie on the lower horizontal edge.

11 Fold the same flap forward.

A good origami artist

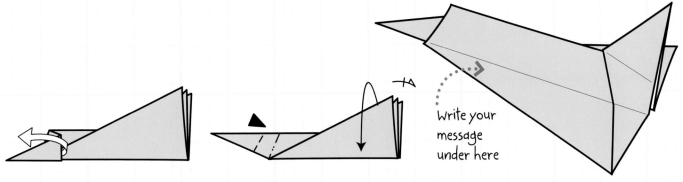

12 Unfold to step 10.

13 Fold the nose section in and out, making the same mountain and valley crease on both sides. Fold the wings down halfway.

14 This creates the completed model.

Write your message under here

MAKE A PERISCOPE

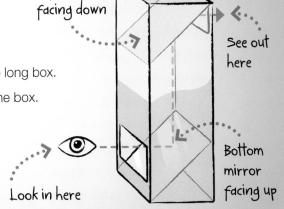

Top mirror facing down

See out here

Look in here

Bottom mirror facing up

A periscope is useful for seeing over high walls. It can be a little difficult to make but is worth the effort.

YOU WILL NEED • Tall juice carton • glue • scissors • two small mirrors (same size) • tape

1 Cut and glue the top of the carton to make it into one long box.

2 Cut a window top and bottom on opposite sides of the box.

3 Place the two mirrors at 45-degree angles facing each other inside and tape in place.

Now look through the bottom window and the mirrors should let you see out of the top.

SECRET FILE

All spies need a way to hide information or to pass secret messages to each other. This model looks like an ordinary wallet, but has a hidden section to hide things in.

MEMORY TRAINING 1

Good spies should have a notebook and pen with them at all times. If this is not possible, the next best weapon in your arsenal is a good memory. You can train your brain to increase your memory power with games like this:

Look at the objects below for 30 seconds. Then cover the objects and see how many you can remember.

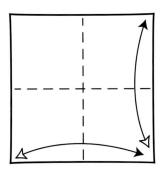
1 Start white side up. Fold in half from side to side, unfold, and repeat.

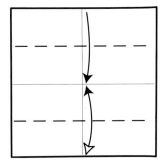
2 Fold the lower edge to the center, crease, and unfold. Fold the upper edge to the center.

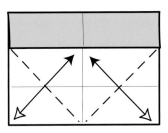
3 Fold both lower corners to the center, crease, and unfold.

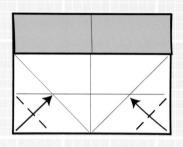

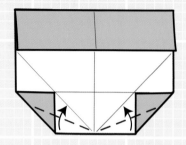

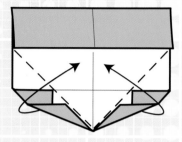

4 Fold both lower corners to the nearest crease.

5 Fold each half of the lower edge to lie on the crease.

6 Refold the lower sections on the existing creases.

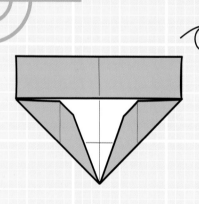

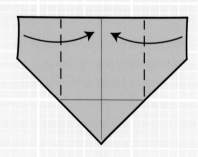

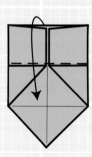

7 This is the result. Turn the paper over.

8 Fold the left and right sides to the center crease.

9 Fold the top section down.

RAIL FENCE CIPHER

A rail fence cipher is another simple way of encoding your message. All you and your contact need to agree on is the number of rows you are using.

The rail fence cipher uses rows of random letters to hide your message. Say your message is "Dr. Evil leaves tomorrow," using a 3-row rail fence cipher you would write it in a V- shape like this:

```
D * * I * A * * T * * R * * * *
* R * V * L * E * V * S * O * O * R * W *
* * E * * L * * E * * M * * O * *
```

Then you would write the letters as they appear in each row to make your message:

D I A T R R V L E V S O O R W E L E M O

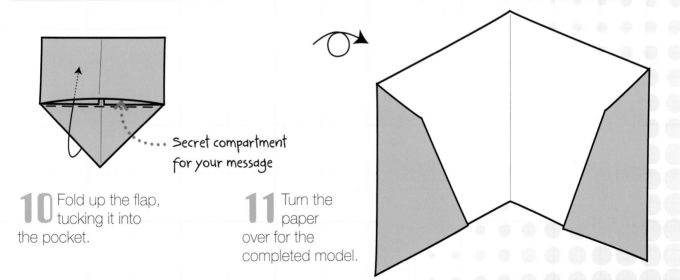

Secret compartment for your message

10 Fold up the flap, tucking it into the pocket.

11 Turn the paper over for the completed model.

COVERT CAMERA

Spies always need cameras—this one folds completely flat, so it is easy to hide it. When you overlap the corner points, then gently spread the paper camera open, it will take the shot with a "click!"

snap!

MEMORY TRAINING 2

Remembering what people look like is a useful skill to have. Being able to give a good description of your suspects is an important part of your mission. There are a number of things you should look for:

What is the color of their hair?

What is the color of their clothes?

Are they tall/short?

What is the length/style of haircut?

Are they carrying anything?

Any there any special features such as a scar or birthmark?

Do they have a beard/moustache?

Is there anything strange about their behavior?

What are they wearing?

Do they walk with a limp?

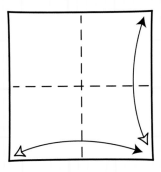

1 Start white side up. Fold in half from side to side, unfold, and repeat.

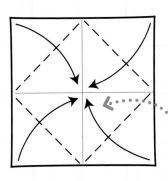

Write your message here

2 Fold all four corners to the center.

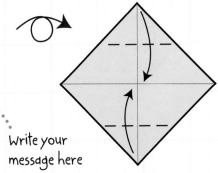

3 Turn the paper over and fold two opposite corners to the center.

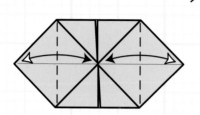

4 Fold the outer corners to the center, crease firmly, then unfold.

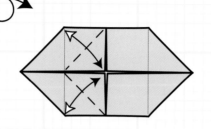

5 Turn the paper over. Fold the corners to the center, creasing where shown.

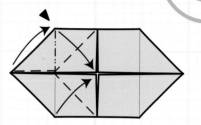

6 Use the creases shown to collapse the paper upward.

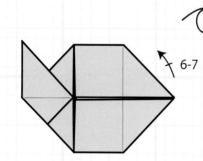

6-7

7 This is the result. Repeat steps 6–7 on the other side.

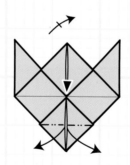

8 Turn the paper over. Open and squash the lower flap. Repeat at the top.

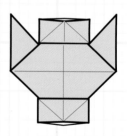

9 This is the result. Turn the paper over.

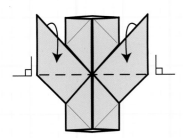

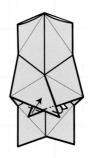

10 Fold the two flaps down at right angles.

11 Fold the model into itself and overlap the middle flaps.

12 Wrap the corner points around the edges to complete the model.

COUNTER SPY

As a spy, you have to be wary of your enemies trying to spy on you. You have to use what is known as counter spy—methods of protecting yourself from your enemies.

To see if someone has been snooping in your room, tape a hair over the crack in the closed door before you leave. Do this at the very bottom, where it is less likely to be spotted. If the door has been opened, the hair will either be broken or pulled from one of the pieces of tape.

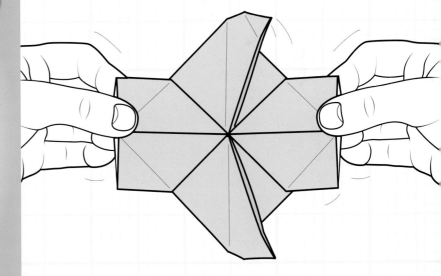

13 Point and shoot the camera. Click!

HAWK ID

The hawk is a symbol of a top-class spy that is used all over the world. Use it to identify yourself in tight situations!

INVISIBLE INK

The best way to hide your message from your enemy is to make it invisible. You can make a simple invisible ink using lemon juice.

YOU WILL NEED • Cotton swab, paintbrush, or feather point • lemon juice • paper • lightbulb or iron

1 Dip your writing tool into the lemon juice.

2 Use this to write your message on a piece of paper. The message will disappear as the juice dries.

To reveal the message, ask an adult to help you heat the paper over a bright lightbulb. Ironing the paper will also work.

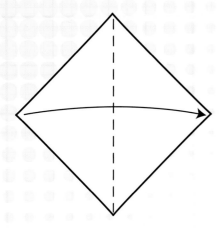

1 Start white side up. Fold in half from left to right.

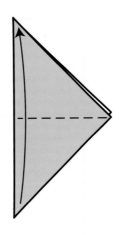

2 Fold the lower corner to the top corner.

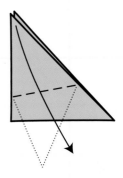

3 Fold the first flap down to the dotted line.

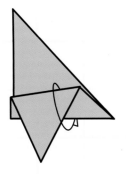

4 Swing the two layers underneath.

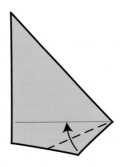

5 Fold the lower right edge to the crease going across.

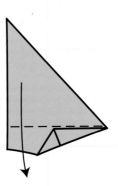

6 Fold the top half downward.

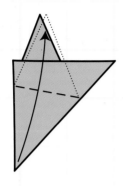

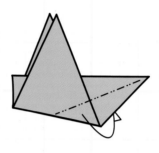

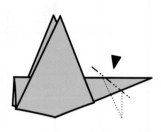

7 Fold the lower corner up so it is slightly to the side of the lower flap.

8 Fold the lower right edge underneath and inside the layers.

9 Press the beak down between the layers.

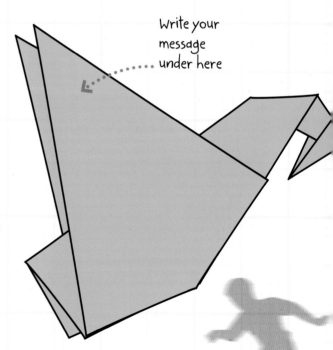

Write your message under here

10 Wrap the end of the beak outside as you fold it backward.

11 This completes the model.

DQG LV KDSSB WR VKDUH KLV VHFUHWV

STEGANOGRAPHY

Steganography means to hide a message (such as a drawing or text) behind something else. This has been a popular way of disguising secrets for thousands of years.

In the past steganography has included hiding messages behind coverings of wax, printing on cloth secretly attached to clothing, and writing in places hidden on the body.

Using steganography, no one else will even know that a message has been sent. A person will receive some sort of "cover" that hides what you really want to say.

A simple method of steganography that you can try is to cover your drawing (or text if you prefer) with paint and crayon. This makes a secret scratch card for your contact. With a bold color or design on the front, no one else will know that a secret drawing or text is hidden behind there as a message.

YOU WILL NEED • Piece of cardstock • black felt-tip pen • wax crayon • poster paint • paintbrush

1 Using the felt-tip pen, put your secret drawing or text on the card (see picture 1).

2 Press down hard with the wax crayon to cover over the message (see picture 2).

3 Load up your brush with poster paint and thickly cover the crayoned part of the message. Cover over the message (see picture 3). Wait for the paint to dry.

4 Deliver your secret scratch card. Your contact can use the edge of a coin to scratch off the layers to reveal the message!

Picture 1
Use black felt-tip pen

Picture 2
Cover with wax crayon

Picture 3
Use heavy paint

SUBMARINE

Nuclear submarines are vital for defense around the world. They can also be used by spies as an undercover way to travel to faraway locations.

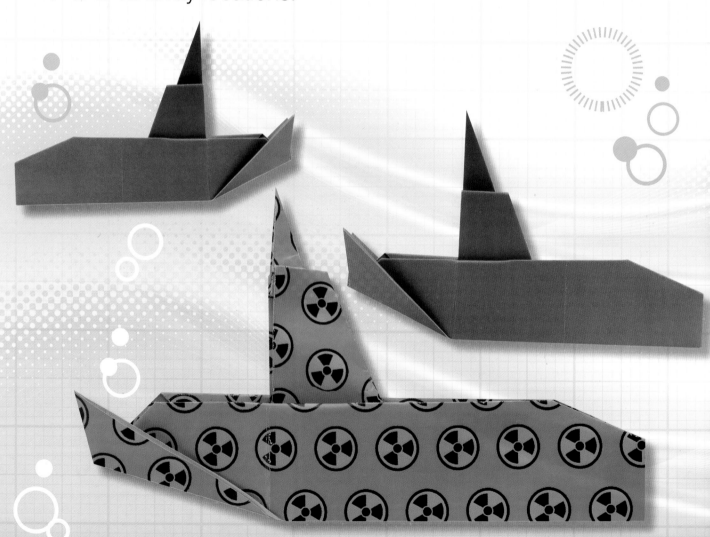

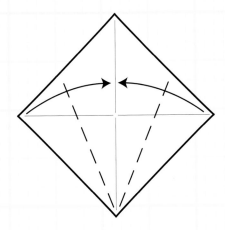

1 Start white side up with the diagonals creased. Fold the two lower edges to the upright center.

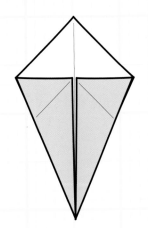

2 This is the result. Turn the paper over.

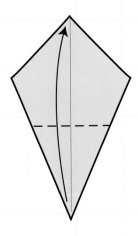

3 Fold the lower narrow corner to the top corner.

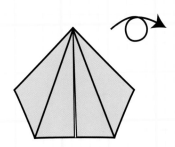

4 This is the result. Turn the paper over.

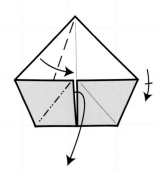

5 Pull down the corner as you fold the white edge to the upright center. Repeat on the right side.

BOOK CIPHER

As long as you and your contact have the same edition of the same book, you can use a book cipher to pass on your messages.

The simplest form of this cipher replaces whole words instead of individual letters. The way it works is by finding the words you want to use in the book by giving the page number it appears on, then the number of the line the word appears on, followed by the number the word is in that line.

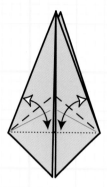

6 Fold each upper edge to the horizontal crease, then unfold.

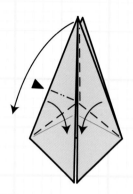

7 Fold the three valley creases at the same time to form a pointed flap, which you flatten to the left to form the mountain crease.

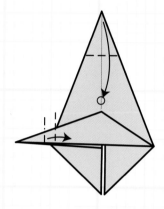

8 Fold the top corner down, then make a pleat on the flap on the left.

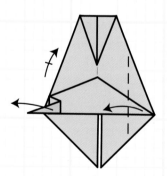

9 Unfold the pleat. Fold the right corner to the center and repeat on the left.

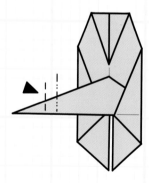

10 Fold the left flap in and then out again.

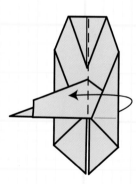

11 Fold the right side of the model over to the left.

EASY DISGUISES

One of the key skills that you can learn is how to disguise yourself. This can help you to blend into crowds, tail someone without being seen (see page 44), or hide from the enemy.

Try these quick and easy disguises:

Wear reversible clothing—handy for a quick change if you need to throw someone off the scent.

Wear a hat.

Put on sunglasses— but only if it's sunny, otherwise you will draw attention to yourself.

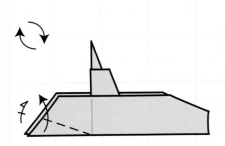

12 Rotate the paper clockwise. Fold the rudders of the submarine upward on both sides.

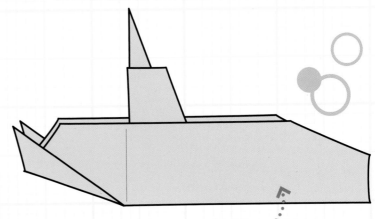

13 This completes the model.

Write your message under here

SKY SPY

A satellite can operate within the atmosphere or outside of it. It can transmit data to Earth and provide close-up images of any part of the world.

TRAILING PEOPLE

A good spy never gets seen. You have to learn to blend into the background like a chameleon. This is especially true when you are following someone. The trick is not to draw attention to yourself. Use the techniques you learned on page 43 to help you.

Here are some basic rules you should follow:

- Don't get too close—you need to stay in the background.

- Don't stay too far back—you might lose the person.

- Stay calm—don't appear too anxious or you'll arouse suspicione.

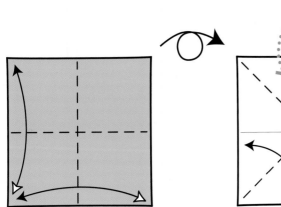

Write your message here

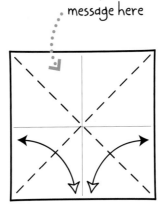

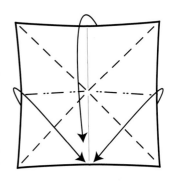

1 With colored side up, crease in half and unfold, both ways.

2 Turn the paper over. Crease and unfold both diagonals.

3 Use the creases shown to collapse the paper into a triangle.

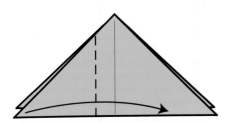

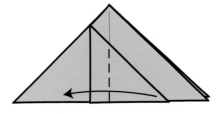

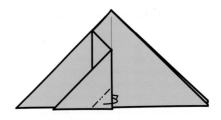

4 Fold a single corner over. The farther you fold it, the taller and slimmer the model will be.

5 Fold the corner back along the upright center.

6 Fold the corner underneath.

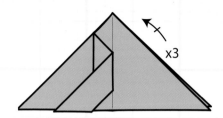

7 This is the result. Repeat on the three other flaps.

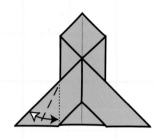

8 Fold the outer edge to the vertical, crease firmly, and unfold.

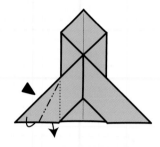

9 Push the edge between the layers.

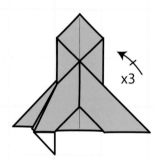

10 This is the result. Repeat on the three other flaps.

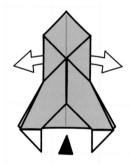

11 Put a finger inside the model and carefully open it out to three dimensions.

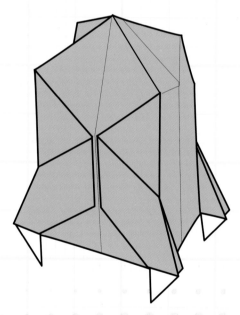

12 This completes the model.

EMERGENCY CODE WORDS

A good spy stays in control at all times. However, there may be times when things do not go as planned. There may be emergencies where you need to pass a quick message to your contact.

You cannot have a long talk; your message needs to be clear and short. You also need to think about how you send your message.

If you are talking directly to your contact, or have called him or her on the phone, are other people listening in? A text message or an origami model may be intercepted.

In order to disguise your message, you should prepare some coded sentences that sound like everyday conversation but, in fact, mean something very different. You can make up your own code words or learn the ones below to share with your contact.

If you are texting or writing these messages, don't forget to first put them into code if you can. You can never be too careful.

I'm going on vacation tomorrow
Await new instructions

Do sheep live in flocks?
You're being followed

I like feeding the ducks
The plan has changed

The weather looks stormy
My cover has been blown

Mr. Doe has left the building
I've run out of origami paper

CRACKING THE CODE

Answers to the codes found at the bottom of the following pages:

Page 10/CODE 1: Z FNNC ROX
"A good spy"—cipher wheel *(see page 15)*

Page 18/CODE 2: NRSGEEGTCUHVEAT
"Never gets caught"—3-line rail fence cipher *(see page 31)*

```
N * * R * * S * * G * *
* E * E * G * T * C * U * H *
* * V * * E * * A * * T
```

Page 22/CODE 3: ━•••/••━/━ •━•/•/━━/•/━━/━•••/•/•━•
"But remember"—Morse Code *(see page 11)*

Page 26/CODE 4: A good origami artist
"A good origami artist"—mirror writing *(see page 19)*

Page 34/CODE 5: (symbols)
"Never gets a paper cut"—symbol cipher *(see page 21)*

Page 38/CODE 6: DQG LV KDSSB WR VKDUH KLV VHFUHWV
"and is happy to share his secrets"—Caesar cipher +3 *(see page 13)*

ACKNOWLEDGMENTS

All designs are by Nick Robinson (except for the Camera, which is traditional). Thanks to Wayne Brown for inspiration and assistance. Nick Robinson's website is www.origami.me.uk

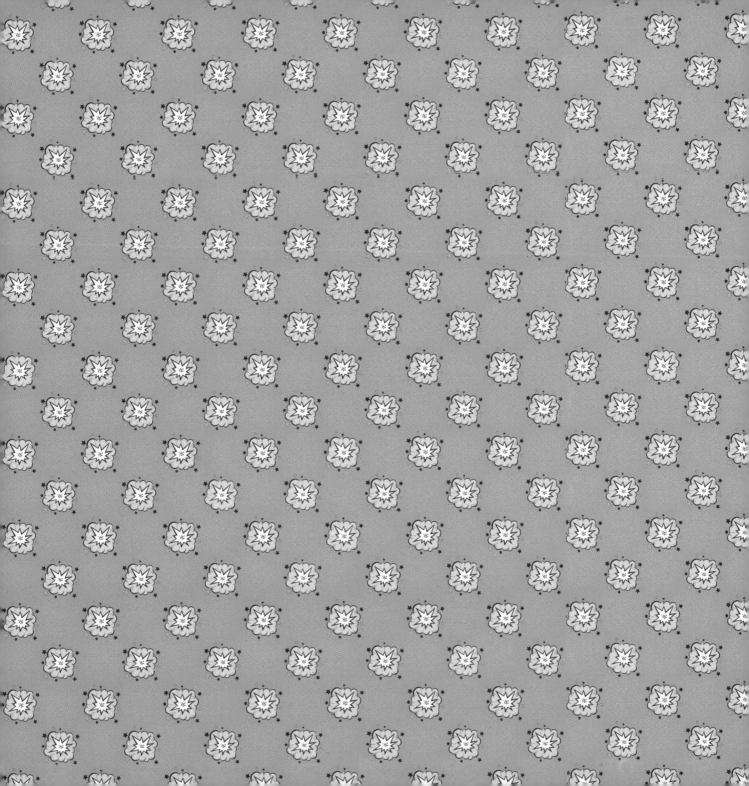

11 01 11001110 11001010 1101 1101 100 11001110 111001110
1110 110110 00111 11000 000111 01 11100110 11101010 110
100 11001110 110010 0001110 11010 00111 11000 000111
01110 11101010 1011 1011 100 11001110 110010 000111
0 00111 11000 00111 01 111000110 11001010 1011 1011 10
01110 110010 0001110 11010 00111 11000 011 000111
01110 11101010 1011 1011 100 110010 110010 0001110 1101
11000 000111 01 11100110 11001010 1011 1011 100 110011
110 0001110 11010 00111 11000 00111 01 11100110 1110101
11 01 11100110 11001010 1011 1011 100 11001110 11101
1110 110110 00111 11000 000111 01 111000110 11101010 110
100 11001110 110010 0001110 11010 00111 11000 000111
01110 11101010 1011 1011 100 11001110 110010 000111
0 00111 11000 000111 01 11100110 11001010 1011 1011 10
01110 110010 0001110 11010 00111 11000 000111 01 11100111
1010 1011 1011 100 11001110 110010 0001110 110110 001
0 000111 01 11100110 111001010 1011 1011 100 110011
110 0001110 11010 00111 11000 011 000111 01 11100111
1010 1011 1011 100 110010 110010 0001110 11010 00111 11000
11 01 11100110 11101010 1011 1011 100 11001110 1110
1110 110110 00111 11000 00111 01 11100110 11101010 0001
11001110 11101010 1011 1011 100 11001110 110010 000111
0 00111 11000 000111 01 11100110 11101010 1011 1011 10
01110 110010 0001110 11010 00111 11000 000111 01 11100111
1010 1011 1011 100 11001110 110010 0001110 11010 00

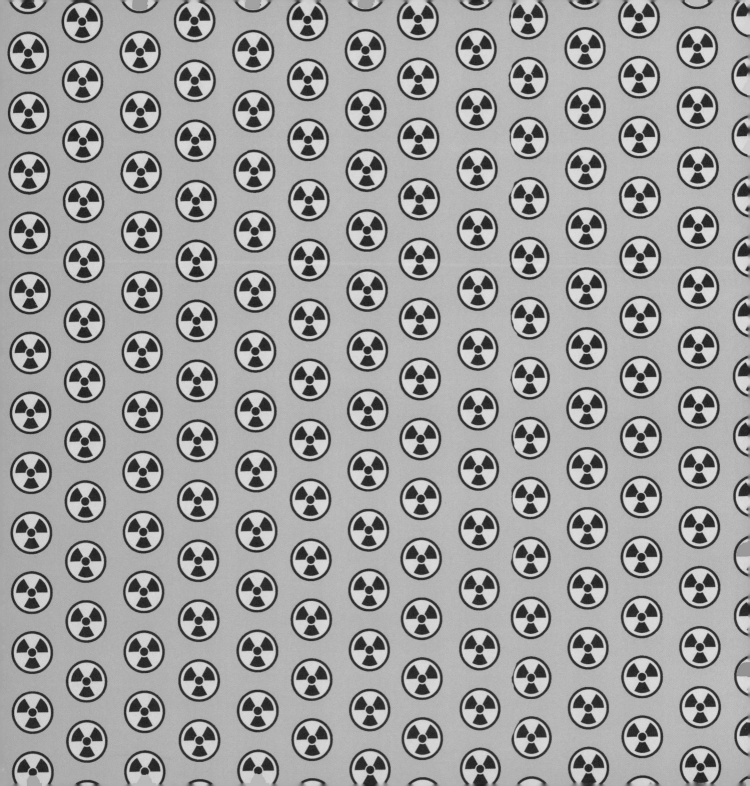